THE
JOKIEST
JOKING SPOOKY JOKE BOOK
EVER WRITTEN . . . NO JOKE!

LOOKING FOR MORE JOKES TO IMPRESS
YOUR FRIENDS AND BUILD YOUR ULTIMATE
JOKEMASTER COLLECTION?

YOU'LL LOVE . . .

THE JOKIEST JOKING JOKE BOOK
EVER WRITTEN . . . NO JOKE!

THE JOKIEST JOKING KNOCK-KNOCK JOKE
BOOK EVER WRITTEN . . . NO JOKE!

THE JOKIEST JOKING TRIVIA BOOK
EVER WRITTEN . . . NO JOKE!

THE JOKIEST JOKING BATHROOM JOKE BOOK
EVER WRITTEN . . . NO JOKE!

THE JOKIEST JOKING PUNS BOOK
EVER WRITTEN . . . NO JOKE!

THE JOKIEST

JOKING SPOOKY JOKE BOOK EVER WRITTEN . . . NO JOKE!

1,001 GIGGLING GAGS ABOUT GOBLINS, GHOSTS, AND GHOULS

JOKES BY **BRIAN BOONE**

ILLUSTRATIONS BY **AMANDA BRACK**

CASTLE POINT BOOKS

NEW YORK

www.castlepointbooks.com

The Castle Point Books trademark is owned by Castle Point Publishing, LLC.
Castle Point books are published and distributed by St. Martin's
Publishing Group.

ISBN 978-1-250-28723-6 (trade paperback)
ISBN 978-1-250-28734-2 (ebook)

Cover design by Rob Grom
Illustrations by Amanda Brack

Our books may be purchased in bulk for promotional, educational, or
business use. Please contact your local bookseller or the Macmillan
Corporate and Premium Sales Department at 1-800-221-7945, extension
5442, or by email at MacmillanSpecialMarkets@macmillan.com.

First Edition: 2023

10 9 8 7 6 5 4 3 2 1

This book is dead-icated to my
Great-Great-Great-Great-Great-Great-
Great-Grandpa Booooooone
(who is a ghost).

CONTENTS

INTRODUCING . . .

What goes bump in the night? Cackles with delight? Laughs it up at an eerie fright? You do, because you're holding in your hands the most spooktacular joke book ever assembled on the subject of witches and werewolves, ghosts and goblins, spookies and ookies, and every other kind of monster. It's *The Jokiest Joking Spooky Joke Book Ever Written . . . No Joke!*

Boo!

Did we startle you? We hope not, because this collection of jokes, jests, japes, riddles, and the ridiculous isn't intended to be all that scary. This is about the lighter side—the silly side—of all those creatures, magical ones and supernatural beings of lore. It's the perfect book for a laugh around Halloween time or any time of year when you want to get a little bit dark . . . but a whole lot funny, too. We've got tricks and treats for you within, so turn the page . . . if you dare!

1
Vampires, Draculas, and Other Bloodsuckers

Why did Dracula go to the doctor?
He was coffin.

What's a vampire's favorite fruit?

A neck-tarine.

Why do vampires avoid biting weather forecasters?

They give them wind.

Why don't vampires use ATMs?

They prefer blood banks.

Did you hear that Dracula was named the best bloodsucker of the year? What a champ-ire!

What do you need to look out for around short vampires?

Your knees!

A vampire vomited, looked down, and disappeared in a poof.

Because acid reflects.

Where does Dracula do all his clothes shopping?

In Cape Town.

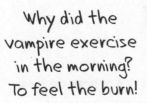

What kind of dogs do vampires prefer?
Bloodhounds.

Does Dracula like the beach?
Only the Cape.

In a ranking of spookiest creatures, where do vampires fall?
Dead last.

Why are vampires so hard to be around?
They have bat breath.

What's pale, has big fangs, explodes in the sun, and wears a cape?

A vampire.

Did you hear Dracula was killed when he went out to dinner?

He chose a stake house.

What do you call a dentist who treats vampires?

Foolish!

What do you get when you combine Dracula and a yeti? Frostbite.

What did Dracula name his boat?
The Blood Vessel.

Where did Dracula sail *The Blood Vessel*?
On Lake Eerie.

What do bats do for fun?
Oh, they just like to hang out.

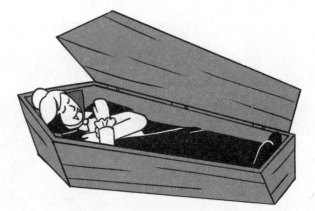

Why did the vampires
suddenly stop sucking blood?
It was time for their coffin breaks.

Did you know that Dracula was a really great crime scene artist?
He was terrific at drawing blood.

How do vampires fix broken teeth?
With toothpaste.

I suggested the vampires sharpen their fangs.
They didn't want to, but then, they had a point.

What vampire can't stop eating chips and dip?
A Snack-ula!

What drinks blood and smells like bacon?
A ham-pire.

**How can you tell that the vampire developed
a sweet tooth?**
The donut shop had all the jelly sucked out of the jelly donuts.

How did Dracula set up his new crypt?
He used fang shui.

**What do you get when you mix flour, eggs, milk,
and a vampire?**
Bat-ter.

Where do vampires get clean?
In the bat-tub.

What did the vampire say when she saw her reflection in the mirror?

"I guess I'm not a vampire!"

Want to hear a joke about a toothless vampire?

Never mind, it's pointless.

The dentist took an X-ray of the vampire's mouth.

And that's how a tooth-pic was made!

Do you think you'll ever see Dracula in the daytime?
Don't count on it.

What do you call vampires in the Mafia?
Fang-sters.

Why did the vampire go to the Red Cross?
Someone mentioned they were handling blood donations.

What kind of
ice cream do
vampires like?
Vein-illa.

What do you get when you
put Dracula on the back of a turtle?
The world's slowest vampire.

What do really tall vampires like?
Giraffes.

Which Ariana Grande song do vampires enjoy?
"Thank U, Necks."

Why did vampires thrive during medieval times?
They lived for the knights!

What drinks blood and quacks?
Count Duck-ula.

Why did the vampire break up with her boyfriend?
He wasn't her blood type.

What's a vampire's favorite sport?
Bat-minton.

What do you call a vampire who eats light bulbs?
A lamp-ire.

The vampire really liked his new dentist.
She made him feel fang-tastic.

What did the vampires make of their new neighbors?
Lunch!

How do vampires stay up all night?
They stay coffin-ated.

What's a vampire's favorite gym class activity?
Casket-ball.

The two vampires knew they'd met their true loves.
It was love at first fright.

Who's a vampire's favorite superhero?
Batman.

Is it easy to take advantage of a vampire?
Sure, they're all suckers!

What do vampires call skateboarders?
Meals on wheels!

Why do vampires always stay close to their families?
Because blood is thicker than water.

What did the vampire say to the mirror?
Nothing!

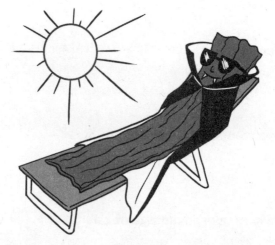

How do you make vampire bacon?
Leave a vampire out in the sun.

What do you call a pair of vampire twins?
Blood brothers.

When did the vampire go to the fang dentist?
At tooth-hurty.

How do you prank a vampire?
Fill your neck with ketchup.

Why did the vampire bite the TV?
She saw that it was a plasma screen.

What's black and white and red all over?
A vampire panda.

Are vampires good at math?
Only if you Count Dracula.

What goes great with a peanut butter Dracula?
A jam-pire!

What kinds of snacks does Dracula prefer?
Bite-sized ones.

How are vampires like stars?

They both only come out at night.

The vampire's business was bound to fail.

Talk about a fly-by-night operation.

VAMPIRE #1: You're a real pain in the neck.
VAMPIRE #2: Hey, thanks!

Why did the vampire read the newspaper?
Apparently it had great circulation.

What pushes blood into your neck?
A vampire on Opposite Day.

What do you get when you cross Dracula with hay fever?
A pollen Count.

What kind of tests do they have at vampire school?
Blood tests.

What sucks blood, has a shell,
and lives underwater?
A clam-pire.

Which vampire never loses?

Dracu-luck!

Which vampire whines?

Pout Dracula.

Why didn't the vampires attack Taylor Swift?

They knew she had bad blood.

What has horns and sucks blood?
A ram-pire.

What do you call a vampire in an RV?
A camp-ire.

Where do young vampires shop?
Forever 21.

Vampires are always trying to get a baseball game going.
They'll even offer to bring the bats!

What does a flexible vampire turn into?
An acro-bat.

What's a vampire's blood type?
Red!

What kind of candy do vampires enjoy?
Drac-olate.

What do you call it when a bunch of vampires race their cars?
A Drac race.

Why did the vampire readily sign the contract?
It was a blood pact.

What grows in the dirt and drinks blood?
A yam-pire.

What do you call a distinguished lady vampire?
A ma'am-pire.

What's the easiest way to stop a vampire?
Shed some light on the situation.

Dracula fell
into a lake.
Now he's
a damp-ire.

What do vampires and computers have in common?
They both run on bytes!

What does a vampire fear most?
Tooth decay.

How are vampires like giant lollipops?
They're all-day suckers.

What do vampires drink when they want something sweet?
Dra-cola.

How do vampires start their letters?
"Tomb it may concern . . ."

Where does Dracula brush his teeth?
In the bat-room.

Why does Dracula both love and hate the butcher?
He loves the blood but hates the stakes.

How does Dracula keep warm?
With a fang-ora sweater.

What do you call a whole bunch of related bloodsuckers?
A fam-pire.

Why did Dracula only have a little blood for dinner?

He had a big lunch.

What is Transylvania, exactly?

It's Dracula's terror-tory.

Why doesn't anybody like Dracula?

He has a bat temper.

To what magazine does Dracula subscribe?

Bleeder's Digest.

What kind of witches like to play croquet?
Wicket witches!

Why can't the young witches go to school?

They were ex-spelled.

What do you call a bunch of witches living in the same house?

Broom-mates.

How do witches play video games?

On a Hexbox.

What's happening when you see a witch at her cauldron? It means trouble is brewing.

How do witches
keep their
skin so gross,
dry, and scaly?
They use
potion lotion.

What's the number one illness affecting witches? Potion sickness.

How do witches make sure their potions are correct?
They use spell-check.

Why are witches so good at operating sports cars?
They know how to drive stick.

A witch covered in sand walks into a restaurant. The waiter says, "We have a menu item named after you." The witch says, "You have a menu item named Beth?"

How does a witch order coffees?
"Hocus mochas!"

Why is it important to remember the name of every witch you meet?
So you can remember which witch is which.

What do you call a witch in possession of lots and lots of potions?
Wrich!

What do you call a brand-new witch?
A baby broomer.

What's worse than getting attacked by a witch?
Getting attacked by two *witches.*

How do you get a witch to kick the bucket?
Throw a bucket at her feet!

What's the first thing a witch does when she checks into a hotel?
She orders broom service.

What do you call a wealthy witch? Richie Witch.

What does witch cereal say?

"Snap, cackle, pop!"

How can you tell if a witch made your lunch?

There are way too many spider eyes.

What do witches drink for energy?

Apple spider.

What do you
call pants
for witches?
Witches' britches.

Why do witches
wear black socks?
To match their hats!

Why do witches get good deals when they go shopping?
They love to hag-gle.

How do you disarm an angry witch?
Tell her she looks bewitching!

Where do witches go on vacation?
Witch-ita, Kansas.

How do witches do their hair?
They use scare-spray.

What do you get when you put a witch in an igloo?
A cold spell.

How do witches send packages?
They use Fed-Hex.

What state is full of witches?
Hex-as.

Why don't witches wear regular hats? What's the point?

How good was the witch's brew?
It was hex-tra special.

Where do witches go when they're sick?
The witch doctor.

How do witches without brooms get places?
They witch-hike.

How do you make a witch itch?
Take away the W.

What's another name for a witch's pointy magic wand?
A hocus-poke-us.

What spell does a witch use to transform someone into a pig?
"Horkus porkus!"

How do witches
count to 100?
With their warts.

Why did the witch explode?
She accidentally rode a boomstick!

I saw a witch picking at her feet.
It made me wonder, is that where candy corn comes from?

What's got six eyes, six legs, and three brooms?
Three witches.

Why do witches wear black hats?
To keep their heads warm.

How did the cat convince the witch
to let it sit on the flying broom?
I don't know, but cats are very purr-suasive.

Where's the best place to learn about witches?
Witch-apedia.

Did you hear about the twin witches who switched places?
It was a witch-eroo!

What kind of knives do witches use?
Witch-blades.

What's the difference between soccer and a coven?
One is played on pitches, and the other is full of witches.

What's a good name for a witch?
Wanda.

What do Australian witches ride?
Broom-erangs!

Why did the witch stop being a fortune teller?
She couldn't see a future in it.

Are witches' brews healthy?

Yes, they're newt-ricious.

How do witches fly?

Witch-ful thinking.

What kind of cereal do witches like?

C-Hex.

What does a cold witch ride?
A brrrrrr-oom.

What happens when a witch gets really mad?
She flies off the handle!

Where do witches find their animal companions?
In a cat-alog.

What happened when the cat
tasted the witch's bitter potion?
It became a sourpuss.

What kind of pet does a sea witch have?
A catfish.

Where else do witches go to find their cats?
Purr-sia.

What did the witch say when she was shopping for cats?
"This one is purrrrr-fect!"

Two witches' black cats got into a fight.
And then they hissed and made up.

The black cat was silent, so the witch took it to the veterinarian.
The doctor gave it a purr-scription.

How do witches get certified?
They take the necessary hex-ams.

Why do witches fly on brooms?
Because vacuums don't hold a charge for very long.

Why couldn't the witch sing at the Halloween party? She had a frog in her throat.

What's the difference between a witch and the letters C-A-S-T-S?
One casts spells, and the other spells "casts."

What are the three kinds of witches?
Good witches, bad witches, and sandwiches.

How do you make a witch stop what she's doing?
Give her an s, so she'll "switch."

How many witches
does it take to
change a light bulb?
Just one.
But she changes
it into a frog.

How do witches say goodnight
to their brooms?
"Sweep tight!"

What's another name for a flying wizard?
A flying sorcerer!

What broomsticks are the fastest?
Vroom-sticks!

WITCH: Where were you when I needed you tonight?
BROOM: Sorry, I over-swept.

Why do witches fly on broomsticks?
It's cheaper than flying in helicopters.

Why did the witch need to put her cat out?
A spell made it catch fire.

How do witches greet each other?
"Warts up?"

Why do witches always carry stools?
In case they need to sit down for a spell.

What do a witch's vessel and the McDonald's mascot have in common?
They're both cauld-ron!

How can you tell a witch is modern?
She rides a Roomba instead of a broom.

What color hair do witches have?
They're brew-nettes.

What do witches get when their shoes are too tight?
Candy corns.

What do witches call their garages?
The broom closet.

Which witch can make the lights go off and on?
A lights witch.

What do you call a witch who likes the beach but is too scared to swim?
A chicken sand-witch.

How come the witch got kicked out of school?
She wasn't cursing enough!

How does a witch write?
In curse-ive.

3
Ghosts, Spirits, and Specters

How do nearsighted ghosts see?
With their spooktacles.

How do you make a ghost blow bubbles?
Give them some boo-ble gum!

Want to hear some jokes about ghosts?
Now, that's the spirit!

What are the scariest things to read?
Boo-ks!

Why do ghosts' sheets hang so low?
So you can't see their boooooots.

What do you call
a ghostly chicken?
A poultry-geist.

Why did the ghost have to wear those spooktacles?
It was short-frighted.

What do ghosts eat?
Whatever they get at the ghost-ery store.

Where do ghosts learn how to haunt?
At boooooooot camp.

What's the tiniest ghost known to man?
The amoe-boo!

Which flowers are the scariest?
Any boo-quet!

What's a ghost's favorite day of the week?
Fright-day!

What do ghosts
wear on their feet?
Boo-ts.

How do ghosts
clean their hair?
With sham-booooo!

A bunch of ghosts formed a choir.
They always sang such haunting melodies.

How do ghosts tell each other when it's safe to haunt a house?
"The ghost is clear!"

Who won the Best Ghost contest?
No body.

How do ghosts listen to music?
With a boooooombox.

What kind of ghost hangs out in the bathroom?

A potty-geist.

What kind of ghost can rhyme and recite verse?

A poetry-geist.

What kind of ghost can make bowls and vases?

A pottery-geist.

What kind of hat would
you see on a European ghost?
A boo-ret.

What kind of road has the most ghosts haunting it?
A dead end!

In what room will you never find a ghost?
The living room.

Did you hear about the city where no people live?
It's a ghost town!

Where do ghosts take vacation?
The Boo-hamas.

Did you hear about the ghost that joined the hockey team?
It played ghoul-tender.

What do you call ghosts that haunt sports stadiums?
Spook-tators!

What happens when you
cross a snake with a ghost?
You get a boo-a constrictor.

Athletes hate playing to a stadium full of ghosts.
They're always booing!

What books are the spookiest?
The ones written by ghost writers.

How often do ghosts show up?
Oh, once in a boo moon.

What do you get when you
cross a ghost and a kitty?
A scaredy cat!

What do ghosts leave in the bathroom?
A boo-poo.

What do you call a ghost primate?
A ba-boooon.

Why did the ghost decide to haunt a tower?
It was in high spirits.

What's white, floaty, and wears sunglasses?
A ghost on vacation.

What do ghosts wear to the beach? Boo-kinis.

What do ghosts put on bagels?

Scream cheese.

Why do ghosts make such spooky noises?

Because they don't know any words.

Why did the ghost get a makeover?

To feel boo-tiful.

How do you get a ghost out of your house?

With scare freshener.

What's a good name for a ghost?
Mona.

Where do ghosts like to sit in restaurants?
In a booooooooth!

What's a ghost's favorite dessert?
Boo-berry pie.

How do ghosts
eat their
hot dogs?
With boo-stard.

What kind of sandwiches do ghosts prefer?

Boo-logna.

What's a ghost's favorite dance?

The boogie-woogie.

How do ghosts open doors?

With spook-keys.

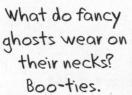

What do fancy ghosts wear on their necks? Boo-ties.

Why do ghosts avoid rain?
It dampens spirits.

Why do ghosts hear so well?
Because they're quite ear-ie.

Why should you always give ghosts a break?
They're just trying to eek out a living.

How do ghosts fly long distances?
They take a scare-plane.

When do ghosts get most of their work done?
They work from Moan-day to Fright-day.

What do ghosts drink?
Le-moan-ade.

Where do little ghosts go when their parents are at work?
Day-scare.

Why are ghosts bad liars?
Because you can see right through them.

Why are ghosts so scary?
It's transparent!

What would you find in a haunted nose?
Boo-gers.

What do you call adult ghosts?
Groan-ups.

Why do ghosts go to football games?
To boo the referees.

What's a ghost's favorite kind of music?
The boos.

What do ghosts eat for dinner?
Spook-getti and meat-boos.

What kind of cupcakes do ghosts like?
Ghost-ess cupcakes.

What's scary, loves honey, and doesn't wear pants?
Winnie the Boo.

What will you find at a ghost barbecue?
Ham-boo-gers!

What's the scariest tree?
BamBOO!

Why are ghosts white?
Because they get so afraid when they see other ghosts!

Try getting a ghost to tell you a secret.
They keep everything shrouded!

How do ghosts make sandwiches?
With dread.

What does a ghost cow say?
"Moooooo!"

What do baby ghosts sleep with?
Their stuffed deady bears.

Where do ghosts get their strength?
At the ghost station.

What do ghosts eat with milk?
Spooky cookies!

Each evening a ghost haunts our town hall.
What a night mayor!

Which city is full of ghosts?
Boo-dapest.

What do you call a ghost that lives in its mama's pouch? A Kanga-boo!

Which country has the most ghosts?

Ghost-a Rica.

Why do ghosts hate gym class?

They don't like to exorcise.

Which painter got even better after he died?

Vincent van Ghost.

Would you find ghosts on the beach?

Only in Maliboo.

What game do baby ghosts love?
Peek-a-boo.

What's the best way to catch a ghost?
With a boooooooby trap.

What kind of trees do tropical ghosts haunt?
Boo-nana trees.

Why are ghosts so effective?
They're just very scare-ful.

Why do ghosts
make great
cheerleaders?
They've got a
lot of spirit!

How do ghosts predict the future?

With their horror-scopes.

Why did the priest go to the haunted house?

He needed to get some exorcise.

What does a ghost rooster say?

"Cock-a-doodle boo!"

What's the slogan of Ghost Nike?

"Just boo it."

What do little
ghosts wear
on Halloween?
Pillowcases.

Who did the ghost take to the prom?
His ghoul-friend.

What do ghosts send their friends when they're on vacation?
Ghost-cards.

What do you call an accidental haunting?
A boo boo-boo.

Why can't you arrest a ghost?
Just try pinning something on them!

Why are ghosts so good at playing instruments?
They can read sheet music.

This house used to be haunted, but the ghost faded away.
He's mist.

I don't know why I married that ghost.
I just don't know what possessed me.

How do ghosts
Keep informed?
They read
the boos-paper.

How do you send a letter to a ghost?

Via the ghost office.

What's scary, floats, and has three wheels?

A ghost on a tricycle.

Where do ghosts buy their sheets?

At boo-tiques.

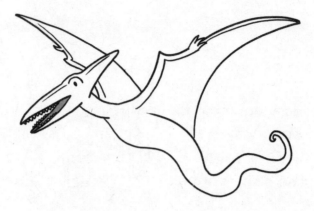

What do you call a ghost dinosaur?
A terror-dactyl.

How did dancing stop the ghost from haunting?
He came down with boogie fever.

How do baby ghosts get clean?
With boo-ble baths.

Why don't ghosts ever pay with credit cards or bills?
They've always got plenty of loose chains.

Do tormented ghosts actually like to scare people?
Sure, with every chain they get.

What did the ghost do when he lost his wallet?
He went haunting for it.

Which ghosts protect the beach?
The Ghost Guard.

What's the biggest fear among shy ghosts?
Public spooking!

How do ghosts say hello to each other?
"How do you boo?"

How does a ghost fire an arrow?
With a boo!

Why did the baby ghost go to the doctor?
To get a boo-ster shot.

What do ghosts put on their cereal?
Evaporated milk.

What does a ship ghost say?
"Buoy!"

How do ghosts haunt other houses without leaving their own?
With Zoooooooom.

Why do spiders like living in haunted houses?
Because ghosts can't walk through their webs.

What's white, black, and blue all over?
A ghost that hasn't learned to move through walls yet.

What do ghosts and toilet paper have in common?
They both come in sheets!

What is scary, white, and constantly goes up and down?
A ghost in an elevator.

I bet this house will be haunted someday.
But then, I'm just specter-lating.

What's black and white and dead all over?
A zombie in a tuxedo.

What kind of weather does a Zombie like?
When it raaaaaaains.

Why don't zombies like jokes?

They've got a rotten sense of humor.

Why don't zombies need jobs?

Because they don't need to make a living.

Why will zombies never give up their pursuit of brains?

Because they're just so dead-icated.

Under what kind of stone
would you find a zombie?
A tombstone.

What did the zombie's grandma say to the zombie?
"My, how you've groan!"

What do you call a bunch of zombies living in a hive?
Zom-bees!

What do zombies like on their mashed potatoes?
Grave-y.

What do you get when you cross
a zombie and a chicken?
A rotten egg.

What are zombies' favorite dogs?
Great daaaaaaanes.

What's a zombie's favorite part of bowling?
The laaaaaaaanes.

**A zombie walks into work. His boss asks,
"Did you get enough sleep last night? You look
a bit dead this morning."**

Why did the zombie fall in love?
The person had beauty and braaaaaaaains.

At what time should you look out for zombies?
Ate o'clock.

What do a butcher shop and a cemetery full of zombies have in common?
They're both full of dead meat.

Why did the
zombie attack
the coffin?
It had an
intense graving.

What do you call a zombie turkey?
A gobble-in.

Why are zombies so unappreciative?
They seem to take things for grunted.

How does a zombie say goodbye?
"It was nice gnawing you!"

What do you call a zombie with lots of kids?
A mom-ster.

What's a zombie's
favorite fruit?
Blood oranges.

Where does a zombie sit?
On its zom-bie-hind.

Why did the zombie cross the road?
To eat the unaware chicken.

What do you call a zombie with a bell?
A dead ringer.

What happened when a
zombie attacked a cow?
It made zom-beef.

On what day is a zombie most likely to attack?
Chews-day.

Why are zombies bad at hide and seek?
You can always hear them groaning.

Why don't zombies attack giraffes?
They don't want to bite off more than they can chew.

You would think zombies would like sausage.
However, they actually think sausage is the wurst.

What candy do zombies love to get on Halloween?
Butterfingers.

What does a zombie call a race car driver?
Fast food!

What do you
call a zombie
with three eyes?
A zombiiie.

Never loan money to zombies.
They're deadbeats!

What game do little zombies love?
Swallow the leader.

Why do zombies hang out in cemeteries?
They just dig them!

How do you make a zombie not smell? Cut off his nose.

Do zombies eat dinner with their fingers?
No, they eat the fingers separately.

What do you call a zombie with no eyes?

A zombe.

What do a zombie and a jack-o'-lantern have in common?

They both have empty heads.

Why did the zombie librarian hang around the cemetery?

The plots.

A zombie tried to enter the house through the window but got stuck. He was in so much pane.

Why are zombies such good students?
They eat a lot of brain food.

Why did the zombie stop eating comedians?
They tasted funny.

How do zombies stay fit?
With Zomba!

What's another name for a zombie cowboy? A boo-ckaroo!

What do you do if a mob of 100 zombies surrounds your house?
You hope it's Halloween.

Do all zombies smell as bad as they look?
A phew do!

Why do zombies never report for work?
They're always feeling so rotten.

Do zombies ever rest?

Of corpse they don't!

What happened to Ray after he met a zombie?

He became an X-Ray.

What did the polite zombie say?

"Pleased to eat you!"

What do you call a
bathroom zombie?
A body in
the potty!

How do zombies cook their meat?
Terror-fried!

What moves oxygen around to a zombie's body parts?
Dead blood cells.

How do you make zombie bread?
With self-rising flour.

How else do you make zombie bread?
With graaaaaaains.

Zombies attacked the poor man and ate his appendages.
He didn't have a leg to stand on.

Why is it so hard to call zombies on the phone?
The line always goes dead.

Who gets the most fed up with people?
Zombies!

What do you call zombies in pajamas? The sleepwalking dead.

Why did the zombie call the morgue?

To see if they offered delivery.

What's the difference between a skeleton and a zombie?

Time!

Who should look out for confused zombies?

Brians!

How do zombies like their sandwiches?

With tomb-atoes.

What kind of money do zombies use?

Cryptocurrency.

All these zombies can't find their way back home.

It's truly a grave problem.

What's a zombie's favorite treat? (Hint: It's not brain food!) Eye candy.

What sandwich do zombies eat?
Limb-burger.

Why was the zombie pleased to be in court?
He thought he'd get a life sentence.

Why don't zombies talk?
Because they're dead!

Why are zombies always moving?
They're trying to get away from the smell of the other zombies.

Why did the
zombie comedian
get booed
off stage?
Because his jokes
were rotten.

Why was the zombie hammering on a tombstone?
They misspelled his name.

What do zombies eat for breakfast?
Raisin Brain!

Where do zombies love to swim?
In the Dead Sea.

Is Zombieland a country?
No, it's a terror-tory.

Are zombies picky eaters?
No, they're gore-mets.

Why do zombies always lurch slowly?
They're too lazy to run.

How did the zombies feel after a night of stalking?
Dead tired!

Did you hear the zombie got a promotion?
He got a position in corpse-orate.

What did the zombie who wanted to travel do?
It joined the Peace Corpse.

What do zombies use their computers for?
Eek-mail.

What goes "Ha, ha, ha, thump!" A zombie laughing its head off.

Are zombies good at math?

Yes, but only die-vision.

Are zombies good at composing

No, but they sure can decompose.

Why don't zombies like pirates?

Pirates are too salty.

What's a zombie's favorite weather?

Cloudy with a chance of brain.

Why did the zombie become a mortician?

To put food on the table.

Why aren't zombies ever arrested?

They can't be captured alive.

Why should you never fight a zombie? Because they'll happily eat a knuckle sandwich.

What's a French zombie's favorite cheese?
Zom-brie.

How do you know if a zombie likes someone?
They ask for seconds.

Why aren't zombies allowed to serve on juries?
They'd always be dead-locked.

How do you know if a mob of undead monsters is about to attack?
You can just feel it in the zom-breeze.

Why do zombies put up fences around cemeteries?
Because people are dying to get in!

What initials do zombies have?
D.K.

Why are zombies so healthy?
Well, they try to eat flesh.

What trees always yield zombies?

Ceme-trees.

What's a zombie's favorite band?

The Grateful Dead.

What do zombies and these jokes have in common?

They're brainless.

Did you hear about the werewolves who wandered into the desert? They were hot dogs.

How does a group of werewolves introduce themselves?
"We're wolves!"

What does a werewolf order at a restaurant?
The waiter.

Where do werewolves stay on vacation?
At a Howl-iday Inn.

What do you get when you leave an old
pair of underwear outside during a full moon?
You get an underwear-wolf.

Did you know there's a holiday to pay tribute to werewolves?
Fangs-giving!

Did you hear about the werewolves who were ashamed of their long dark hair?
They wore gloves to cover it up.

What's the difference between
a dog and a werewolf?
One pants and the other wears pants.

What do you call a werewolf on Christmas? Santa Claws.

Where do werewolves keep their clothes?
In their claw-set.

Why are werewolves good at stirring?
They always bring their own whiskers.

In what city would you find a lot of werewolves?
Howllywoof!

What happened when the werewolf swallowed a clock?

He got ticks!

What would you get if you gave a werewolf an unlimited train ticket?

You'd get a where-wolf.

What would happen if you gave a werewolf a time machine?

You'd get a when-wolf.

What do you call a werewolf with a strong attention to detail?

An aware-wolf.

Jeremy hated turning into a werewolf.

It always meant putting his life on paws.

But was Jeremy a good werewolf?

Sure, he was a howling success!

Do werewolves
like chicken
fingers?
No, they
prefer human.

What did the skeleton say to the werewolf?

"Bone appétit!"

What's as sharp as a werewolf's fang?

The werewolf's other fang.

How can you tell if werewolves like your joke?

They howl.

What's big, ugly, and hides in a dark room?
A werewolf with a migraine.

Did you hear about the werewolf who swallowed a clock?
Now she's a watchdog.

What kind of mail do famous werewolves get?
Fang mail!

What do you get if you cross a werewolf and a kangaroo?
A fur coat with pockets.

What can you get from a were-sheep?
Woooooooool.

What kind of werewolf has no teeth?
A gummy-were.

How do werewolves smell?
Bad. They smell bad.

What's scary, hairy, and bounces?
A werewolf on a trampoline.

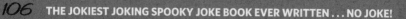

Why do werewolves chase their tails?

To make ends meet.

How's the life of a werewolf?

Ruff.

How do werewolves eat their food?

They wolf it down.

What did the werewolf say when he stubbed his toe? Owwwwwwww!

What do you say when a werewolf leaves?
"Doggone!"

How do you stop werewolves from howling outside?
Bring them inside.

Why don't werewolves ever offer the moon a bite?
Because it's already full.

What kind of
werewolves make
the best nurses?
Care-wolves.

What kind of werewolves have the biggest, unblinking eyes?
Stare-wolves!

Did you hear about the werewolf that attacked the jouster?

It was a bite in shining armor.

Where can you find a lot of werewolves?

In Hair-izona.

What's a werewolf's favorite holiday?

Howl-oween.

Which werewolves
are the most
fashionable?
Wear-wolves.

What kind of jackets do werewolves wear?
Fleas.

What kind of math do werewolves excel at?
Howl-gebra.

Why are werewolves so big and hairy and ugly?
Because if they were small and round, they'd be Skittles.

What do were-cows howl at?
The mooooooon.

What kind of cologne do werewolves wear?

Brute.

**What's the difference between a forest
and a werewolf?**

One is full of owls, and the other is full of howls.

What happened to the bird who met the werewolf?

It became shredded tweet.

What happened to the little dog who met a werewolf?
It was terrier-fied!

Which werewolves wear the hippest clothes?
Streetwear wolves.

What do you call a really great werewolf song?
A fanger!

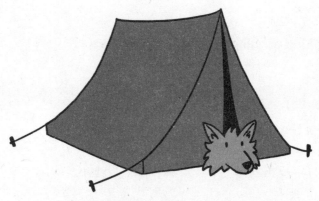

Where do werewolves sleep
when they're out in the woods?
Pup tents.

What do werewolves sing on New Year's?

"Auld Fang Syne."

What happened to Reese when he met a werewolf?

Reese? Is pieces.

How can you tell when werewolves are happy?

If their tails are wagging and they don't want to bite you.

Where do werewolves meet to dance?
At the hair ball.

Did you hear about the werewolves
with stomachaches?
It must have been someone they ate.

What made the werewolves so upset?
They got mooned!

Where will you always find a werewolf?
In the barking lot.

**What should you always bring home for your
werewolf roommate?**
The doggie bag.

How do fancy werewolves eat their prey?
With knives and forks.

How can you tell when werewolves are really old?
When they bite you, their teeth stay behind.

Where will you never find a werewolf shopping?
At the flea market.

Why do werewolves
have thick coats?
Fur protection!

What do healthy
werewolves
eat in the morning?
Smooooooothies!

**What's the difference between a werewolf
and potatoes?**
You can't mash a werewolf.

**What kind of monster can easily make changes
in his life?**
A self-aware-wolf.

Who can point out a werewolf?
A there-wolf!

What do you call a horse werewolf?
A mare wolf.

How does a werewolf have five parents?

Well, it's got one maw and four paws.

Why might werewolves go home early?

If they are dog-tired.

What do you call a speedy werewolf?

Furry in a hurry.

Cross a Christmas tree with a werewolf and what do you get?
A Douglas fur.

Once transformed, how long do you stay a werewolf?
Fur-ever!

Which trees do werewolves enjoy?
Dogwoods!

What do werewolves like on their pizza? Pupperoni!

Why didn't the werewolf go see a therapist?
He wasn't allowed on the couch.

What do you call two werewolves?
Pair wolves.

How do you make a were-chicken?
Wait for a fowl moon.

How do you make a silly werewolf?
Wait for a fool moon.

What do you call a group of young werewolves?
A litter!

Who's the most even-handed werewolf?
A fair wolf.

Why is a werewolf a good pet?
A werewolf is a dog that can walk itself!

Turning into a werewolf?
That's got to be a real hair-raising situation.

Why did the werewolf have to face facts and see a dentist?
Because the tooth hurts.

Who's in charge of Werewolfville?
The mayor wolf.

What magical creatures smell the best?
Scentaurs.

What grades did the Creature from the Black Lagoon get in school?

All seas.

What do swamp monsters like to snack on?

Marsh-mallows.

How do monsters take their coffee?
With lots of scream.

You can't trust the swamp monster.
There's something fishy about him.

Did you hear what happened when a bunch of monsters trampled a city?
It was a monster mash.

Did you hear about the nervous sea monster?
It was a shaken kraken!

Frankenstein's monster is
so good at gardening.
It must be his green thumb!

What do monsters eat for breakfast?
Scream of Wheat.

What do sea monsters eat for lunch?
Fish and ships.

How do you greet a five-headed monster?
"Hi, hi, hi, hi, hi!"

What stresses out sea monsters?
Current events.

Why did the gross creature live in a swamp?
It wanted to live in the slimelight.

The Creature from the Black Lagoon was just too busy to scare anyone.
At work, he was swamped.

Where do sea creatures go when they're feeling sick?
The dock-tor.

What's a great gift for
an eight-armed monster?
Four pairs of gloves.

Who won the monster beauty pageant?
Nobody!

Why do monsters see psychics?
For their horror-scopes.

What kind of vehicles do monsters drive?
Monster trucks.

Which monster
is the best dancer?
The boogeyman!

Which monster can spit on walls?

The loogie-man.

Which monster jokes around too much?

Prank-enstein!

How do you make a rib eye steak?

Combine a skeleton, a Cyclops, and some meat.

Why did the
two-headed
monster get all As
in school?
Because two heads
are better than one.

Why do Cyclopes always get along with each other?
They see eye to eye.

What should you give a monster who is trick-or-treating?
Whatever it wants!

KID #1: I once saw a giant monster.
KID #2: That sounds like a tall tale.

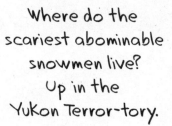

Where do the scariest abominable snowmen live?
Up in the Yukon Terror-tory.

Monsters often eat chicken.
But only if they're in a fowl mood.

The Cyclops made a terrible teacher.
He only had one pupil!

How do monsters use mouthwash?
They gargoyle it.

Which side of a sea monster
has the most scales?
The outside!

Where can you
find an ogre?
Ogre there!

How do monsters take their eggs?
Gargoyled.

How did Frankenstein's monster feel when he was lit by lightning?
Shocked!

How do monsters wish each other a happy holiday?
"Scary Christmas!"

Who's skinny
but deadly?
The Slim Reaper.

What game do kid monsters love to play?

Hide and go shriek!

What do little monsters ride at the amusement park?

The scary-go-round.

Why are monster basketball courts always wet?

They keep dribbling.

How do you get to the second story of a haunted house?

Take the mon-stairs!

What should you do if a monster comes to your front door?

Go out the back door!

What should you do with a green monster?

Wait until it ripens.

How do you know if there's a monster in your backpack? You can't zip it up.

What's the best way to talk to a monster?
From as far away as possible.

Which monster has two mouths?
The one with two heads.

What do you get if you cross a flea with a monster?
A scared dog.

What's big, green, and goes "beep-beep-beep"?
A monster stuck in traffic.

How do monster stories start?
"Once upon a slime . . ."

Did you hear about the five-legged monster?
His pants fit him like a glove.

When do giant monstrous snow creatures go to the doctor?
When they're feeling abominable.

Why was the abominable snowman bald?

He lost his hair in a hair raid.

What did the right ear of Frankenstein's monster say to his left ear??

"Hey, we live on the same block!"

I tried to explain math to Frankenstein's monster but he didn't get it.

What a blockhead!

What do you get when you
cross a Bigfoot with a pumpkin?
A sas-squash.

Frankenstein's monster can never wake up calmly.
He always awakens with a bolt.

Where do monsters get their hair done?
At the ugly parlor.

Where can you find giant snails?
At the end of a giant's fingers.

How can you tell if a monster has a fake eye?
It'll come out in conversation.

What kind of
monster grows
in the woods?
Frankenpine.

What kind of monster is green, tiny, and can be wiped on your brother?
The booger-man.

What cereal do monsters use to make treats?
Rice Creepies.

Who's dumb but deadly?
The Dim Reaper.

What's something eerie?
A monster with five ears!

Who's too uptight to harvest souls?

The Prim Reaper.

What's written on the tombstone of Frankenstein's monster?

"Rest in Pieces."

MONSTER #1: Why'd you name your dog Frost?
MONSTER #2: Because Frost bites.

What did the art teacher say about the sculpture Frankenstein's monster's made?

The teacher thought it was a monster-piece!

How come they don't have Bigfoot in Europe?

Because he's known as Bigmeter there.

Which monster discovered electricity?

Benjamin Frankenstein.

Who cleans the sea monster's house?
The mermaid.

Why did the
monster get braces?
It had an ogre-bite.

Frankenstein's monster squeezed his girlfriend too hard.
It was a powerful crush.

Who brings monster babies?
The Franken-stork.

Which sea monster has a giant tongue?
Moby-Lick.

How do abominable snowmen get around?
Icicles!

Which monster is the biggest slob?
The Loch Mess Monster.

Dr. Frankenstein was never lonely.
He was so good at making friends.

How can you help a hungry monster?
Give it a hand!

What do abominable snowmen order at the drive-through?
Hambrrrrrrgurs.

Why was the monsters' Thanksgiving potluck so boring?
Everyone brought monster mash.

What do monsters leave in the toilet?
Spooky dookie!

How do you know which
part of a blob is the head?
Tickle it in the middle
and see which end laughs.

What does Bigfoot
wear on his feet?
Big shoes.

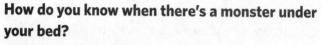

How do you know when there's a monster under your bed?

It moans.

How else do you know when there's a monster under your bed?

It leaves a note asking for more delicious dirty socks!

Why did the monster paint himself sixty-four colors?

So it could hide in a crayon box.

What's bigger than an abominable snowman?

An abominable snowman's dad.

How do sea monsters hear each other from miles away?

Herring aids.

What do ogres eat for breakfast?

Ogre-t.

What spooky thing likes s'mores?

The Graham Reaper.

What does the Grim Reaper eat for breakfast?

Golden Grims.

What happens when you cross death with marshmallows?

You get the Grim Peeper!

Why do sea monsters always know exactly how much they weigh?

They have access to scales.

Frankenstein was the pilot on my last trip.
It was a terror-flying experience.

What monster is in the best shape?
The abdominal snowman.

What's green, lurches, and complains?
Frankenwhine.

Why did the monster eat a light bulb?
Because it wanted a light snack.

What did Frankenstein's monster say to his bride?
"I was dying to meet you!"

Why didn't the monster cross the road?
And be called a chicken?

What cookie do monsters love?
Ladyfingers.

Never play catch with a 5,000-pound monster.
They're just too heavy.

How come you never see a monster hiding in a bush?
Because they're just so good at it.

Why did the sea monster decide to start haunting on land?
He needed a breath of fresh air.

MONSTER #1: That's the ugliest baby I've ever seen!
MONSTER #2: Thanks, I'm so proud of it.

The sea monster was on an all-seafood diet.
Whatever he sees, he eats.

How does a sea monster text?
With its shell phone.

Where does a sea monster keep its money?
In a riverbank.

How can you communicate with a sea monster?
Drop it a line.

The abominable snowman has a little store, but he doesn't take credit cards.
Only cold, hard cash.

What does the abominable snowman eat for breakfast?
Frosted Flakes!

What wakes up monsters in the morning?
Coff-eek!

What do angry sea monsters create?
A comm-ocean!

Who's the smartest monster of them all? Frank-Einstein.

$e=mc^2$

How did the kid know it was time to get a haircut?
When Bigfoot took his picture.

What do sea monsters put on their bagels?
Lochs.

Why does no one dress up as the boogeyman at Halloween?
Because no one likes the boogeyman!

Why doesn't the boogeyman scare babies?
Cribs are just too small for him to crawl under!

What's green, hideous, and covered in chocolate?
A bon-bon-ster.

What comes out of the nose of Frankenstein's monster?
Frankenslime.

What's big, green, and is worth ten cents?
A Frankendime.

Why does Bigfoot always leave footprints?
Because his feet are filthy.

How do you make Bigfoot into a bear?
Shave him. (You'll make him a bare.)

Why are most monsters covered in wrinkles?
Well, have you ever tried to iron a monster?

What do you call a monster with no neck?
The Lost Neck Monster!

What's a monster's favorite bean?
A human bean.

What happened to the platypus that ran afoul of the monster?
It became a splatypus.

Why did Frankenstein's monster get indigestion?
He bolted down his food.

How do ogres say goodbye?
"Fear well!"

Why do
skeletons burp?
They don't have
the guts to fart.

Are skeletons rebels?
Sure, they're
bad to the bone!

Which spooky creatures weigh the most?
Skele-tons.

Why did one skeleton start a fight with another skeleton?
It had a bone to pick.

A girl walked into a party and saw three skeletons.
"Gosh," she said, "It's dead in here."

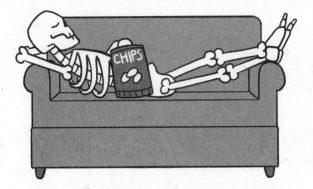

What do you call a skeleton
that won't attack?
Lazy bones!

A zombie and a skeleton walk into a restaurant and the waiter kicks them out. They ask why, and the waiter says to the skeleton, "You're gutless," and to the zombie, "You're dead meat!"

A skeleton walks into a coffee shop and says, "Can I have a cup of water and a mop?"

How do skeletons organize their scare missions?

They call each other on the tele-bone.

What instrument do skeletons play in monster bands?

The trom-bone.

What's the scariest thing you can get on Halloween?

A toothbrush!

Are skeletons good learners? Sure. They keep an open mind.

What do you call a skeleton that won't wake up?
Bone tired!

What do skeletons say when they leave?
"Bone voyage!"

You're scared of skeletons but who are skeletons scared of?
Dogs!

How do you find
a missing skeleton?
Hire Sherlock Bones.

When is it bad luck to see a black cat?
When you're a mouse.

What's a five-letter word with no vowels (and full of bones)?
Crypt.

Why can you always trust a skeleton's recommendations?
They know all the good joints!

Why did the skeleton keep
its head in a freezer?
It was a numb-skull.

Why do skeletons
drink milk?
It's good for
the bones!

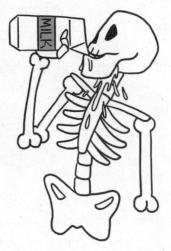

Don't look now but there's a skeleton here.
It's inside of you!

Why couldn't the skeleton fall in love?
It didn't have the heart.

Did you hear about the skeletons who went to a restaurant for lunch?
They ordered spareribs.

How do little skeletons get to school?
On the skull bus.

How does a skeleton feel in the cold?
Chilled to the bone.

Did you hear about the skeleton who always laughed?
It was made up entirely of funny bones.

What did the skeleton do when it lost its head?
It called a headhunter.

Where do skeletons keep their hands?
In a handbag.

What do skeletons do when they lose a hand?
They get a new one at the secondhand store.

How did Old West skeletons send messages?
Through the Bony Express.

Where would you find the Temple of the Skeleton?
On the side of its head.

What kind of choices do skeletons prefer?
No brainers!

Who won the skeleton bodybuilding competition?
No body!

Why are skeletons so relaxed?
Nothing gets under their skin.

Who works on a ghost ship?
A skeleton crew.

How did the skeleton so naturally scare others?
It's just what it was bone to do.

What kind of art do skeletons make?
Skull-ptures.

Why did the skeleton go to the mechanic?
It needed some body work.

Why can't skeletons be in the church band?
They don't have any experience with organs.

So what do skeletons play instead?
The xylo-bone!

Skeletons shower, but they never use a towel.
They always come out bone dry.

Why was the skeleton buried in the yard?
Because the dog got ahold of it.

Why did the skeleton's head cross the road?
To get to the other spine.

What TV show do skeletons love?
Game of Bones.

What do you call an artificial skeleton?
Phony boney.

How do you greet a French skeleton?
Bone-jour!

Did you hear about the skeleton who read too many jokes?
It laughed its head off!

Why did the
invisible man fail
his job interview?
He didn't know
where he saw
himself in five years.

What really spooked the invisible man?

His shadow.

Why does the boogeyman live in bedrooms not graveyards?

Because graveyards are full of scary skeletons!

Why do kids love to go trick-or-treating?

Because there's a boogeyman in their bedrooms!

What kind of jewelry does the headless horseman wear?

A neck-less.

What no longer bothers the headless horseman?

Headaches!

That mummy was a terrible liar.

Look how quickly its story unraveled!

What do you call
a mummy with
a stopwatch?
An old timer.

I cook and my mummy friend always cleans up afterward.
Mummies are so good at wrapping things up!

How did the mummy spend its weekend?
It just laid around.

DOCTOR: Mummy, you need a vacation.
MUMMY: Why, doctor?
DOCTOR: You're all wound up.

What do you get when you
cross a honey-maker and a mummy?
A mumble bee.

What did the little undead do when it ran into the ancient tomb?

It ran right for its mummy.

How did the mummy react to the boring party?

It was bored stiff.

Why didn't the mummy have any friends?

It was so wrapped up in itself.

What kind
of music do
mummies like?
Wrap.

What was King Tut's mother's name?
Mummy!

Which mummies are the stickiest?
The ones who wrapped themselves in candy wrappers.

What do mummies put on their toast?
Preserves.

Does a rotting mummy smell good?
No, it sphinx!

What do you call a giant mummy?
Gauzilla.

What do you call a friendly mummy?
A chummy mummy!

What's a good name for a mummy?
Murph!

My friend told me to not kill the spider and to just take it out instead.
We went to a movie!

What would you call an undercover arachnid?
A spy-der!

How tall is a spider?
Eight feet!

What would happen if spiders were horse-sized?
If one bit you, you could ride it to the doctor's office.

Why do spiders spin webs?
Because they can't knit.

What does a spider do when it gets angry?
It goes up the wall.

What did the spider call his mom's sister?
Tar-aunt-ula!

What's the scariest type of spider?
The terror-antula!

I smashed a spider crawling across the floor with my shoe.
How dare he steal my shoe!

Why do spiders eat corn?
So they can make cobwebs.

What did the spider say to the fly on Halloween?
"The web is the trick and you're the treat!"

What's red, black, and dangerous?
A red and black spider!

What do you get if you cross a tarantula with a rose?
Who knows, but don't smell it!

Where do spiders seek medical advice?

Web MD.

How do spiders stay in shape?

They go to spin class.

Why are spiders so nervous?

Because they're hanging on by a thread.

What could you call a nervous creepy crawly?

A jitterbug.

Why did the woman flee from a giant spider?

Because the spider spied her!

Did you hear about the spiders who are engaged?

They want a big June webbing.

Why do spiders eat corn?

So they can make cobwebs.

What are spider webs good for?
Spiders!

Why are spiders so charming?
They've got the world on a string.

On which day should you watch out for spiders?
Websday.

How can you find out which creepy crawlies are the worst?
Look it up on a website.

Why do spiders love Halloween?
Because it's the one day everybody likes them!

What do you call a blob with no hands or feet?
A blob!

What's the blob's full name?
Blobert.

What kind of racing do blobs do?

Drag racing.

Who steals teeth in the night?

The Tooth Scary.

Why would it be foolish to fight an army of squids?

They're well-armed.

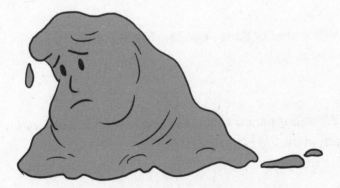

Why can't blobs ever win?
They're constantly defeeted.

Who prepared the Bride
of Frankenstein for the ball?
Her scary godmother.

What kind of dance can Mothra attend?
A moth ball.

What happened to the guy who couldn't keep up on his payments to his exorcist?
He was repossessed!

What do you call a toilet wearing a fuzzy seat cover?
A costume potty!

What kind of math do you do on Halloween?

Arithma-tricks!

How do you make a pumpkin shake?

Tell it a spooky story.

I had a rabbit sitting on my shoulders, but it ran away during a ghost story.

The story was so scary that it made the hare on the back of my neck stand up.

Last night I had a dream
about a frightening horse.
It was a nightmare!

What party treat
is positively evil?
Deviled eggs!

The new cemetery in town is great.
It's earning grave reviews!

What's another name for a decorated headstone?
A cos-tomb.

How much do tombstones weigh?
A skele-ton.

What do you call a smiling jack-o´-lantern?
A pump-grin!

What's the best way to watch a scary movie?
On a flat scream TV.

What's the best food to eat on October 31?
Halloweenies!

Why are bikes scary?
They're full of spooks!

It's not just a pretty pumpkin . . .
It's gourd-geous!

How was the Halloween party?

Spooktacular!

What kind of area would you need to fix a smashed jack-o'-lantern?

A pumpkin patch.

I just don't believe her story about winning the pumpkin-carving contest.

It's full of holes.

How do you make squash?
*Take a pumpkin, throw it in the air, and wait
for it to "squash"!*

What do you call related pumpkins?
Pump kin.

Did you hear about the haunted pancake house?
That place gives me the crêpes!

What do you call the juiciest,
biggest pumpkin in the patch?
A plump-kin.

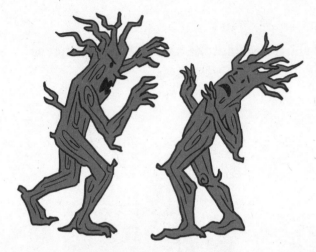

Which forest is so scary it frightened itself?
The Petrified Forest.

What dance do cheesemakers do at Halloween?
The Muenster Mash.

Why did the girl get sick at the haunted house?
It was far too spew-key.

Bulls hate haunted houses.
They're cow-ards!

What do you call a split pumpkin?
A cracked-o'-lantern.

What do you call a bag of pumpkins?
A sack-o'-lanterns.

The jack-o'-lantern was smiling but it was actually sad.
It felt so hollow inside.

How do you hold a Halloween disguise together?
With mask-ing tape.

What's a better name for a horror film?
A boo-hoo-movie.

What's the scariest breakfast cereal?
Dreaded Wheat!

Where are cemeteries always located?
In the dead center of town.

What's a good name for a mortician?
Ceme-Terry!

What do you get when a
sheep comes back to haunt?
A ban-sheep.

What do you get when you cross a
monster with a friendly dog?
A ghoulden retriever.

Why did the boy monsters want to go to the school dance?
They heard there would be ghouls there.

A goblin tried to lure my dog.
It was pet-rifying!

Where do ghouls learn to be scary?
At ghoul school.

Which flowers are planted
around haunted houses?
Mari-ghouls.

How do you get rid of a ghoul?
Spray it with Ghoul-Gone.

What position would a spooky creature play in hockey?
Ghoulie!

What do ghouls eat for dinner every night?
Ghoul-ash!

What's another name for monster barf?
Ghoulash.

Did you hear that the bank fired its goblin teller?
The goblin kept coming up short.

Where do monsters buy their cookies?
From Ghoul Scouts.

Which monster will eat all your snacks?
Goblins!

On which day besides Halloween do the ghouls come out?
On April Ghoul's Day!

On what day do banshees scream the most?
Moan-day.

What's the greatest play ever written about monsters?
Romeo and Ghoul-iet.

What should you do with a blue goblin?
Try to cheer it up.

Which monster loves porridge?
Ghouldilocks.

Why did the ghoul have surgery?
To have its ghoul stones removed.

What flowers do banshees like best?
Mourning glories.

**KID #1: Did you go see that banshee movie
in the theater?**
KID #2: No, I saw it on a screaming service.

What should you do with a red ghoul?

Apologize for embarrassing it!

Why do demons and ghouls hang around together?

Because demons are a ghoul's best friend!

Did you hear about the goblin with eight arms?

It got a job as a handyman.

A goblin popped its nose
right off its face. Why?
It wanted to see what made its nose run.

What do banshees drink?
Lem-moan-ade.

What kind of monster party never has enough food?
A goblin party!

Where do ghouls stay on vacation?
At a gobl-inn.

What kind of salads do goblins eat?
Gob salad.

Who fixes shoes for ghouls?
A cobblin' goblin.

TURKEY: [Gobbles]
GOBLIN: Were you talking to me?

What's yellow, spooky, and grows in a field?
Corn on the goblin.

What's a goblin's favorite day of the week?
Fright-day!

Where do Southern goblins live?
In North and South Scare-olina.

Three goblins were arrested for throwing a party.
They had thrown it into the lake.

What do you call a goblin with a broken foot?
A hobblin' goblin,

What do ghosts
wear on their
ghost legs?
Boo jeans.

What kind of makeup do ghouls wear?

Mas-scare-a.

What's spooky and made of cabbage?

Ghoul-slaw!

What do you get when you cross a banshee and a detective?

Sherlock Moans.

What's thin, round, and spins around a ghoul? A ghoula hoop!

What do they put on their ice scream?
Ghoul Whip.

Who's the hungriest monster?
A gobblin'.

What's another name for a store's Halloween section?
A back-to-ghoul sale!

Did you hear the banshee bought her own haunted house?
Now she's a home moaner!

What do monsters eat for dessert? Ice scream.

What do banshees do for extra credit at school? They work as hall moan-itors.

Why did the banshee marry a pirate?

So she could wail around the seven seas!

Where do banshees catch a train?

At the wail-way station.

What would you call a painting of a banshee?

Moaner Lisa.

Why are banshees
great at tennis?
They make
a good old racket!

Why was the banshee not allowed in the haunted house?

Because "shee" had a "ban."

How can you tell if a banshee is around?

Well, have you ever heard of a quiet banshee?

What do you get when you give some banshees guitars?

They form a band-shee.

What's a tiny
monster's favorite
kind of music?
Rock 'n' troll!

What do ghouls drink on Halloween?

Ghoul-aid.

What do ghouls order at a restaurant?

Choking pot pie.

What do you call a clever bridge dweller?

A droll troll.

What should you avoid if you don't want to pay the troll's toll?
Avoid the troll booth!

Did you hear about the goblin that got its left arm and left leg cut off?
Well, now it's all right.

Why did the troll army lose?
They were ogre run!

What's mischievous, gross,
and made of bread?
Trolls!

What kind of product do monster
sheep provide?
Ghoul.

What do you call the troll in charge?

In con-troll!

Why do ghouls like ice cream?

Because it's ghoul-icous!

What is the hardest thing to sell to a ghoul?

Life insurance!

Why did the ghoul bury the trophy in the cemetery? Because it wanted it engraved.

What did the ghouls eat at the barbecue?
Hand-burgers.

Where can you learn more about ghouls?
Ghoul-gle.com!

Want to hear a joke about a troll?
It's a little funny.

"I need a new pointy hat,"
the witch said bluntly.

"Long ago, a werewolf bit me,"
he said rabidly.

Spooky Swifties

"The vampires got her!" he said mistakenly.

"I hope I don't run into any skeletons," he said gravely.

"Let's go tame a full-moon creature,"
she said wolfishly.

"That vampire exploded so hard smoke is coming off of it," he fumed.

"That's not *really* Dracula," she discounted.

"This has been a grave undertaking," he said cryptically.

"That's the last time I try to touch a zombie," she said offhandedly.

"I can split demons in two," she imparted.

"Gremlins must have done it!" he implied.

"A spirit transported me from the couch to the chair," she said, visibly moved.

"I've just been stabbed in the chest!" the werewolf said half-heartedly.

"Let's send through an electric current," said Dr. Frankenstein amply.

"Demons can be robbed," she said improbably.

"A dog bit me!" he said gnawingly.

"It's time for the second funeral," she rehearsed.

"Yes, I agree to smell like a dog," the werewolf assented.

"I've just been staked in the heart," the vampire said pointedly.

"I keep destroying things with my hands,"
said the monster bashfully.

"I'm going to get a hair transplant,"
said the werewolf baldly.

"Those silver bullets can't hurt me,"
said the werewolf blankly.

"I'm halfway up Bigfoot Mountain!" he alleged.

"This brush isn't helping my hair one bit," the werewolf snarled.

"I just swallowed a fishing lure," the sea monster said with baited breath.

"I've only enough carpet for the haunted house's hall and landing," she said with a blank stare.

"I'll be there to see the trolls," she said shortly.

"That's a very large sea monster,"
she said superficially.

"I'm going out with a mermaid tonight,"
he said sedately.

"I keep shocking myself," she said, revolted.

"The giant sea creature died," he wailed blubberingly.

"They had to remove a bone from my arm," the skeleton said humorlessly.

"Ships ahoy!" the sea monster said fleetingly.

"I don't want a second helping, thank you," said the zombie manfully.

"All brooms are useful!" said the witch, making a sweeping generalization.

"Use your own hairbrush," the werewolf bristled.

"Get out of my hair," was the werewolf's brush-off.

"I don't like being stepped on by monsters!"
he said flatly.

"Yes, I'm *that* strongly built," said the vampire soberly.

"I am not a fraidy-cat," the witch's companion purred.

"There are only two Draculas instead of three,"
he recounted.

Wicked What-Am-I's

I'm scary, but in the end, I'm sweet.
What am I?
Halloween.

**From the head down to the toes,
I flow through every living thing.
Some faint when they see me.
What am I?**
Blood.

I am a home for one, but a danger for others.
I am silky smooth, but I am never desired.
What am I?
A spiderweb.

If you're afraid of it, it isn't doing its job. What is it? A scarecrow.

With pointy fangs I sit and wait.
With piercing force, I deliver fate.
Over victims, I proclaim my might.
I can eternally join with a single bite.
What am I?
A vampire.

I have a name,
but it's not mine.
You don't think
about me while
in your prime.
People cry when
I catch their sight.
Others lie with me
all day and all night.
What am I?
A tombstone.

You may see this hairy creature by the light
of the moon.
You can start running, but it will catch up soon.
What is it?
A werewolf.

I have no body and am just a head, yet my smile
lights up the night.
What am I?
A jack-o'-lantern.

Ghosts and vampires, eagerly awaiting,
will come looking for me on a dark autumn
night, and with a ding or a rap,
I'm given over to them. What am I?
Halloween treats.

**What do mummies, zombies, vampires, goblins,
and witches all have in common?**
The letter i.

**I am a body with a leg, an arm, and a head, but I don't
have flesh or eyes.
What am I?**
A skeleton.

**I'm tall when I'm young, short when I'm old, and every Halloween, I stand up with the pumpkins.
What am I?**
A candle.

**He's old, has a white beard, and performs magic, but he is completely absent on Halloween.
Who is he?**
Santa Claus.

I am wrapped,
but I am no gift.
I am kept neatly
in a chamber, and
archeologists find
me interesting.
What am I?
A mummy.

A place where the living will move.
A shrine under the sun.
Greeted by the morning's crest,
to rest when the day is done.
What is it?

A graveyard.

If you see one flying around, you'd better
be careful at night — some turn into
something that will give your neck a nibble.
What are they?
Bats.

**Empty as a space and scary as a ghost,
I return each night.
What am I?**
Darkness.

I am known to be bad luck when
you see me in the dark.
You will certainly never hear me bark.
What am I?
A black cat.

She who built
it sold it. He who
bought it never
used it. She who
used it never saw it.
What is it?
A coffin.

You're in a room. There's a ghost in the room.
But you're all alone.
How is this possible?

You're the ghost.

Twisted Tongue Twisters

A zombie zonked out because it needed some zzzzzz's.

Seven spindly spiders spin spooky silk speedily.

If two witches were to watch two watches, which witch would watch which watch?

Which witch wished which wicked wish?

Horribly hoarse hoot owls hoot howls of horror in Halloween haunted houses.

Dracula digs dreary, dark dungeons.

He thrusts his fists against the posts and still insists he sees the ghosts.

If big black bats could blow bubbles, how big a bubble would a big black bat blow?

Ghostly ghouls gather gleefully to golf on ghostly golf courses.

Creepy crawly critters crawl through creepy crawly craters.

Gobbling gargoyles gobble gobbling goblins.

Professional pumpkin pickers are prone to pick the plumpest pumpkins.

Transylvanian tree trimmers are trained to trim the tallest Transylvanian trees.

Looming Limericks

There was a monster hunter named Paul,
Who defeated nine werewolves one fall.
Nine is such a good score,
But he tried for one more.
He lost. You can't win them all, Paul.

There once was a thingamajig,
Like a whatsis, but three times as big.
When it came into view,
It looked something like you,
But then it turned into a pig.

There was a young witch named Rose,
Who had a large wart on her nose.
She had it removed,
And her appearance improved,
But her glasses slipped down to her toes.

There was a young werewolf from Maine,
Who gave everybody a pain,
Though what was the cause,
Except for his claws,
I could never quite fully ascertain.

[On a Tombstone]
Here used to lie the body of Mr. Green,
He hasn't been seen since last Halloween.

Knock-Knock!
Who's there?
Boo.
Boo who?
Well, are you a
ghost or an owl?

Knock-knock!
Who's there?
Troll.
Troll who?
Troll-ing right along!

Knock-knock!
Who's there?
Norway.
Norway who?
There's Norway I'm staying out here on this spooky night!

Knock-knock!
Who's there?
Interrupting Zombie.
Interrupting Zomb —
Braaaains!

Knock-knock!
Who's there?
Gremlin.
Gremlin who?
Gremlin in my tummy—I'm hungry!

Knock-knock!
Who's there?
Zombies.
Zombies who?
Zombies make honey, and others don't.

Knock-knock!
Who's there?
Zombie.
Zombie who?
The zombie who's
going to break
down your door!

Knock-knock!
Who's there?
Frida.
Frida who?
Frida spiders,
aren't you?

Knock-knock!
Who's there?
Deluxe.
Deluxe who?
Deluxe Ness Monster!

Knock-knock!
Who's there?
Lucretia.
Lucretia who?
Lucretia from the Black Lagoon!

Knock-knock!
Who's there?
Spooky owl.
Spooky owl who?
Who!

Knock-knock!
Who's there?
Dismay.
Dismay who?
Dismay seem funny to you, but there are monsters out here!
Help!

Knock-knock!
Who's there?
Dog.
Dog who?
Doggone it, open the door! There's a werewolf after me!

Knock-knock!
Who's there?
Ears.
Ears who?
Ears a few too
many monsters
out here!

Knock-knock!
Who's there?
Esther.
Esther who?
Esther any ghosts in there?

Knock-knock!
Who's there?
Canoe.
Canoe who?
Canoe come trick-or-treating with me?

Knock-knock!
Who's there?
Window.
Window who?
Window we get to go trick-or-treating?

Knock-knock!
Who's there?
Mustache.
Mustache who?
I mustache you to let me in, because I'm a vampire.

Knock-knock!
Who's there?
Luke.
Luke who?
Luke at that
full moon!

Knock-knock!
Who's there?
Goblin.
Goblin who?
Goblin your Halloween candy in one night will give you a stomachache!

Knock-knock!
Who's there?
Dozen.
Dozen who?
Dozen anybody want to give me candy?

Knock-knock!
Who's there?
Fangs.
Fangs who?
Fangs for turning me into a werewolf!

Knock-knock!
Who's there?
Voodoo.
Voodoo who?
Voodoo want to go trick-or-treating?

Knock-knock!
Who's there?
Mummy.
Mummy who?
You don't recognize your own mummy's voice?

Knock-knock!
Who's there?
Invisible man.
Hey, long
time no see!

Knock-knock!
Who's there?
Warlock.
Warlock who?
Warlocked out
of the house.
Let us in!

Knock-knock!
Who's there?
Police.
Police who?
Police come outside and defend me against this zombie horde!

Knock-knock!
Who's there?
Orange.
Orange who?
Orange you glad I'm not a vampire?

Knock-knock!
Who's there?
Juicy.
Juicy who?
Juicy that vampire turn into a bat?

Knock-knock!
Who's there?
Berry.
Berry who?
Berry glad it's almost dawn; there are werewolves out
 here tonight.

Knock-knock!
Who's there?
Muffin.
Muffin who?
Muffin is going to stop me from getting away from
these monsters!

Knock-knock!
Who's there?
Dubai.
Dubai who?
We need Dubai some garlic if we're going to keep running
into vampires.

Knock-knock!
Who's there?
Freak.
Freak who?
Freak candy please
— it's Halloween!

Knock-knock!
Who's there?
Olive.
Olive who?
Olive these zombies are after me—let me in!

Knock-knock!
Who's there?
Pumpkin.
Pumpkin who?
Pumpkin you fill up that ball and we can play outside!

Knock-knock!
Who's there?
Sharon.
Sharon who?
Sharon my Halloween candy with you tonight!

Knock-knock!
Who's there?
Needle.
Needle who?
Needle little more help from an exorcist to expel these ghosts?

Knock-knock!
Who's there?
Noah.
Noah who?
Noah good place to hide from these zombies?

Knock-knock!
Who's there?
Dishes.
Dishes who?
Dishes a very scary haunted house!

Knock-knock!
Who's there?
Skeleton.
Skeleton who?
No body's home.

Knock-knock!
Who's there?
Wanda.
Wanda who?
Wanda suck your blood. I'm a vampire!

Knock-knock!
Who's there?
Yam.
Yam who?
I yam getting out of this spooky graveyard!

Knock-knock!
Who's there?
Autumn.
Autumn who?
We autumn run, zombies are on the move!

Knock-knock!
Who's there?
Atomic ache.
Atomic ache who?
Atomic ache is going to happen if you eat all that Halloween candy at once.

Knock-knock!
Who's there?
Leaf.
Leaf who?
Leaf everything behind—we've got to escape from these monsters!

Knock-knock!
Who's there?
Gruesome.
Gruesome who?
Gruesome since last I saw you!

Knock-knock!
Who's there?
Wendy.
Wendy who?
Wendy freaks come
out at night,
we should be inside!

Knock-knock!
Who's there?
Howl.
Howl who?
Howl long before you let us in?

Knock-knock!
Who's there?
Ben.
Ben who?
Ben waiting for candy. Trick-or-treat!

Knock-knock!
Who's there?
Howled.
Howled who?
Howled are you now?

Knock-knock!
Who's there?
China.
China who?
China see the invisible man, but no luck.

Knock-knock!
Who's there?
Icy.
Icy who?
Icy a lot of people out here, but not the invisible man.

Knock-knock!
Who's there?
Athena.
Athena who?
Athena ghost!

Knock-knock!
Who's there?
Defense.
Defense who?
Defense around de cemetery wasn't enough to keep de zombies in!

Knock-knock!
Who's there?
Apollo.
Apollo who?
Apollo dirt out here where that grave used to be. Gulp!

Knock-knock!
Who's there?
Goat.
Goat who?
Goat to a sunny spot to avoid vampires!

Knock-knock!
Who's there?
Theodore.
Theodore who?
Theodore of the sea monster is so bad you can smell it all the way up here on land!

Knock-knock!
Who's there?
Ooze.
Ooze who?
Ooze that
monster over there?

Knock-knock!
Who's there?
Oscar.
Oscar who?
Oscar a vampire to come in and they will!

Knock-knock!
Who's there?
Levy.
Levy who?
Levy borrow a clove of garlic to vend off this vampire!

Knock-knock!
Who's there?
Tyson.
Tyson who?
Tyson garlic around
your neck to
repel vampires!

Knock-knock!
Who's there?
Hannah.
Hannah who?
Hannah me that silver. I see a werewolf.

Knock-knock!
Who's there?
Headless horseman.
Well, there goes the neigh-borhood!

Knock-knock!
Who's there?
Ivana.
Ivana who?
Ivana suck your blood!

Knock-knock!
Who's there?
Jaclyn.
Jaclyn who?
Jaclyn Hyde!

Knock-knock!
Who's there?
Ice cream.
Ice cream who?
Ice cream every time I see a ghost!

Knock-knock!
Who's there?
Howie.
Howie who?
Howie gonna hide all this candy from my brother?

Knock-knock!
Who's there?
Ghost.
Ghost who?
Ghost stand in the open door and give me some Halloween candy!

Knock-knock!
Who's there?
Cement.
Cement who?
Cement to scream when she saw Dracula, but she fainted instead!

Knock-knock!
Who's there?
Thumping.
Thumping who?
Thumping scary is right behind you!

Knock-Knock!
Who's there?
Lena.
Lena who?
Lena little
closer so I can
see your neck.

Knock-knock!
Who's there?
I didn't knock. Those are my knees—I'm scared!

Knock-knock!
Who's there?
Turin.
Turin who?
Turin to a vampire on Halloween!

Knock-knock!
Who's there?
Fangs.
Fangs who?
Fangs for opening
the door,
I'm a vampire!

Knock-knock!
Who's there?
Vampire.
Vampire who?
Vampire State Building!

Knock-knock!
Who's there?
Witch.
Witch who?
Which what?

Knock-knock!
Who's there?
Witch.
Witch who?
Witch you would let me in now!

Knock-knock!
Who's there?
Werewolf.
Werewolf who?
Here wolf!

Knock-knock!
Who's there?
Boo.
Boo who?
Sorry, I didn't
know a sad
ghost lives here.

Knock-Knock!
Who's there?
Boo!
Argh, a ghost!

Knock-knock!
Who's there?
Boo.
Boo who?
Well, you don't have to cry about it.

Knock-knock!
Who's there?
Boo!
Boo who?
Don't cry. I'm just a ghost!

Knock-knock!
Who's there?
Gladys.
Gladys who?
Gladys Halloween!